HOW TO DEAL A DIFFICULT HUSBAND

Secrets To Dealing With A Narcissistic Sociopath Husband

By

Claire Robin

Copyright

All rights reserved. No part of this publication **How To Deal With A Difficult Husband** may be reproduced, stored in a retrieval system or transmitted in any form or by any means - electronic, mechanical, photocopying, recording, and scanning without permission in writing by the author.

© **2020 by Claire Robin**

ZeroNever Publishing House

USA | UK | Canada

Table of Contents

Copyright 2

Introduction 4

CHAPTER 1: Who is a difficult husband? 7

CHAPTER 2: Characteristics Of A Narcissistic Sociopath Husband 16

CHAPTER 3: Making a Decision 25

CHAPTER 4: Surviving A Problematic Marriage 30

CHAPTER 5: Making It Work With Your Difficult Spouse 40

CHAPTER 6: Making Marriage With A Narcissist Sociopath Work 48

CHAPTER 7: Can Marriage To A Narcissist Sociopath Husband Ever Get Better? - How To Make It Work 51

CHAPTER 8: Guide To Being The Submissive Wife . 54

Conclusion 60

Introduction

A difficult husband can succumb, and a narcissist sociopath can be tamed; it all depends on how you approach them. There are ways of handling different kind of men, including the one you married. This book will help you find out how.

It is hard to say that a difficult husband is a good husband; having a sociopath as one makes the case even worse. However, the situation will never be as bad as when you are married to a narcissistic sociopath; you will feel like you should give up, but his manipulations will keep you spellbound. He may be a good man, but not a good husband. I know that a man is the head of the home; yes, he is, but he is not the only member of the family. The failure of some men to understand this has brought many well-meaning wives under pressure. Many homes break because of difficult men.

It can be tough to stay married to a narcissistic sociopath husband. If you are not secure, you will lose your self-confidence and peace. If there are children involved, they may believe their father is right and build their lives based on the dictatorship and cunningness of their father.

If the children are grown, they may get to hate the unyielding attitude of their father. Or on the other way round, the children may get to believe they are not loved. This thought alone can push kids to seek solace outside the home, thereby making mistakes that could have easily been avoided.

Maybe you have noticed this trend in your home. Are you unhappy? Are you finding it difficult to have even a little control over your home? Read on to be sure your husband is not a complicated kind.

This writing will help you know if your husband is just generally difficult or if he acts the way he does because of a personality problem (i.e. he is a narcissist sociopath). It will also help you know how to handle your difficult husband, depending on the cause of his difficulty.

CHAPTER 1: Who is a difficult husband?

A difficult husband is one who oppresses his family, whether consciously or unconsciously. Is that definition too harsh? I don't think so. Now, see this with me. No one feels entirely happy in a home where a difficult husband **rules.** Here, the husband does not lead; he rules. The sad part is that he rules by manipulating everyone to play according to his rules.

Men have their ego, and they do more than you can imagine protecting it. Now, before jumping into a conclusion that your husband is difficult, you have to be sure that he is genuinely being that and not just being a man. The table below will help you know if your husband can be classified into any of the classes of difficulty.

When he is just a man	When he is difficult
He makes decisions on his own every once in a while	He does not consider your opinion about anything
He pulls back for a day to see how	He is always drawn back and does not care

valued he is	what you or the kids think about it
He earnestly forgets to pay the energy bill	He makes up stories to shift the energy bills to you. He may find some lies to cover for it, but sometimes, he does not even care to say anything.
He tries to call in whenever he is late for the family dinner	He comes late and is unconcerned about how you feel. If you ask, he raises an issue.

Signs Your Husband Is Difficult

It is possible to be married to a man that is not a sociopath. This man may just be difficult at his level, and difficult men have some similarities with a sociopath husband. Because of this, you may be tempted to think that he is a sociopath. Let us consider the characteristics of a difficult man. We will also look at the attributes of a difficult sociopath husband.

We may never exhaust the list of the signs of a difficult husband. Difficult husbands will always have different attributes based on their personalities. However, let us consider the general characteristics of a difficult husband.

a) He does not consider anyone

An inconsiderate man will be a dictator husband, and this is the general term for a difficult husband. A husband that does not take his time to consider how his actions and decisions will affect his family is difficult, and the only type of marriage and home a man like this can produce is a toxic one.

Without God, there can be no joy in that home. There will be consistent strife in the house and lack of unity. The man may not even take his time to provide as much as the family needs to survive. This kind of marriage is certainly not the kind you wanted.

b) He is insensitive

A man in this class is a bit subtle. This man cares about the home but just can't understand why you feel he does not love you. I mean, he comes back home at midnight every time because he is working overtime to provide for the home. He finds it difficult to understand why the kids carry a sulked face when he comes back home. I mean, he is providing for the home and this reason, only, he should walk into a consistently happy home.

These husbands earnestly love their families; the only problem they have is that they do not just know how to show it past provision. A man in this class believes when he gets back from work, he should see you dressed in sexy lingerie waiting for him to get a good sex and afterwards crash. The idea of having a romantic dinner is undoubtedly foreign to him since he believes everyone will be more satisfied when they eat at home.

c) He is oblivious

Okay! This is a huge problem. I mean, how can a man continually forget his wedding anniversary and the children's birthday? What do we call such a man? Hmmm! This may be a very annoying part of your husband, but it should not be a cause for alarm. Many women have been married to forgetful men and they in one way or the other got through it.

Though this character may not be very intentional, it is disturbing to the parties involved. A man who continuously forgets important dates and details about the family will lead his family members onto believing he does not care about them. This is a painful fact.

d) He plays the victim's role

This habit can be very irritating. Imagine a man who hurts you with his actions and claims he is hurting in a way you can't understand. Are you his mother? I know men hurt, and I also know when they use the word 'hurt' to get their way. This kind of man is not just tricky, he is manipulative, and this is not healthy for your marriage.

e) He always needs something in return for every favor

This kind of man can be so challenging to manage. Love should be sacrificial, and marriage is the bed on which love is expressed;

so why is he always trying to get something back for every favor he did you? Yes, he helped your sister when she was in a financial problem, but why is he trying to create a dubious means by for you to repay? This attitude cannot be it. If he does this, then he is part of the problem; no marriage can be sweet when the husband is difficult.

f) He is abusive

This is the height of it and before you go on defending your husband (though it's good you do), remember that not all abuses are physical. Some are mental, emotional and sexual. Does your husband have sex with you against your will; then it's an abuse. Do not think that marriage makes it less intolerable. If you have a man that always blackmail and abuse you emotionally, know that man is difficult. There is no way to find joy around such a person. So what should you do with a man like that? We will discuss it soon; hang on!

g) It is difficult to receive anything from him

Is your husband's fist made of iron? That means you have to subject it to enough panel-beating or a very high temperature before you can get a dime. This man is no easy to manage. He is your husband, and because of that, his properties and finances automatically become yours. If he is not comfortable with this, he can argue with his great-grandfather in the grave.

Sharing your body and entire life with a man who feels he can give you his biological properties (sperm), but not his financial assets is difficult. So, you can know if your husband is difficult if you need to inflict yourself with excess planning accompanied by fasting and prayers before receiving a thing as little as a wristband from him.

h) His word is always a law that you must obey

He gives orders! Who does that? Are we in the army barracks? Hush! These men do not just understand that we also have a say. Does your husband do this? If yes, then I'm sorry. I know what you have been going through all these years.

Having a dictator as a husband is no pleasing experience. He will make it seem as though you are so negligible. Wives with this kind of husbands say they feel belittled whenever their husbands throw their orders around. According to them, the feeling gets worse when he does it outside the home.

Yes, men have the authority (part of it), and we women are their **significant** other; they do not have to order us around to feel like they are in charge. After all; we both know they are not. Remember, you are his significant other. If your opinion were not necessary, you would have been called his insignificant other. If most men understood this, the world would have been a better place.

i) He is easily angered

"That is his temperament; he is choleric, and he just can help it"… Many women say this to defend their husbands' irresponsibility. If it is just his temperament, he should have learnt how to control it before taking you to the altar and saying "yes, I do".

Displaying such level of indiscipline is not a mistake; neither is it just a sensitive issue you should defend. Since he is now a husband, then it is imperative upon him to be responsible first for his actions and then for is home. And the failure to do that will only make his house a less enjoyable place to stay.

j) You can't pray for your daughter to marry a man like him.

Think of this; if you were opportune to run a background check on the man that your daughter will be bringing home, will you say give your consent after finding out he is just like your husband? Some of us will say yes, while many of us will say no. I know our daughter's husband will not be perfect (except your baby girl will be marrying an angel), but it will be more difficult to say yes to a marriage you see will lead your child to the same predicament.

Our kids are precious, and if you cannot wish a thing for your kid, what makes you think it is right for you? Think about it. If his kind is not right enough for your daughter, that is because there is something awkward about him.

CHAPTER 2: Characteristics Of A Narcissistic Sociopath Husband

Who is a narcissistic sociopath

A narcissistic man is proud of so many egos. A sociopath may have some unresolved issues, but he uses this excuse to manipulate people. This kind of man is extremely conscious of his social appearance; he is charismatic and believes he is the best. Having this kind of as a husband can make life far from being beautiful if the wife does not know how to manage appropriately. Marrying a narcissistic sociopath is the perfect description of what it means to be married to a difficult husband.

I added this segment not to convince you that there is no good man out there; no. Many good and strong men strive to be the best they can be for their families but are also bold enough to apologize for their failures and weaknesses. We know these men, and we love them sincerely for their virtue.

This segment is to help women know that they can be in a problematic marriage without knowing. This situation is common for the newly wedded whose eyes are still very much clouded with the love they feel for their sociopath husband. Do not worry; if you realize your marriage has been stressful or toxic, you can follow our tested, trusted and all-sufficient guide to help you live a sweet life despite being married to the "narcissistic sociopath".

How to know a narcissistic sociopath husband

The surest way to know a manipulative husband is by listening to your guts. If your gut tells you that all is not right about the relationship; believe it. It does not matter whether you can find a tangible reason or not. After all, it is always so difficult to find a concrete reason when your husband will not stop at anything to play with your intelligence and make you feel like you are being too curious and distrusting by asking questions.

Do not forget that sociopaths are usually so sweet and cute; and sometimes, they will put on the boyish countenance to get you to fall (and you have been falling so far). However, before you can tell if he is a narcissist sociopath, you should know the individual characteristics of the two personality disorders:

When he is a sociopath

1. He has this charm

He believes he is cute and genuinely, he may be. But many people are drawn to him because of his appeal. At first, you will think that he is so sweet until you realize he is manipulating you. Manipulation is not a difficult task for this man as he always has the right words and the proper lies to apply when needed. With him, you will easily mistake the truth for a lie and vice versa.

2. He is a beautiful liar

Has a person ever told you lies that got you crying out of pity? If no, then you haven't met a sociopath yet. This guy is one that lies as quickly as blinking his eyes. He has no hindrance, and he never lacks the lies. You ask him about a thing; he will make up a sweet honest-sounding lie that will make you feel wrong for the asking.

He manipulates with his lies and uses them to get anyone he wants. What about getting money? That's where his strength lies; he can make you pay his rent, school fees, buy medicine for his cat, and even add some feeding allowance without having a second thought.

3. Jeez! His self-worth can fill the whole room

This guy does not believe he has faults; in fact, he thinks he is the best in everything. He has this overwhelming self-worth, and this makes him not so teachable. You can never beat the arrogance of that kind of man.

4. He is a sweet leech

The kind of work that we do is too low for a sociopath. Remember he is better than everyone and lives the life of a celebrity; so how does he afford this lifestyle? By leeching onto people. Since he is a professional liar, this is not difficult to accomplish.

5. He has low emotions

Sociopaths are not so familiar with emotions; that is why they do not display them. The only emotions they feel are the basic ones which are: anger, sadness and happiness. Anything more than this will be too complicated for them to handle. This is the reason they do not understand why people feel the way they do.

6. He easily gets bored

Boredom comes natural for a sociopath. It can make him indulge in risky and self-destructive lifestyles just to add the missing spice to his life. He is dauntless and can easily take chances that an average person would not dare.

7. He is dramatic

This guy is right; he can make an innocent person guilty within a split second. That is the reason you end up apologizing to him for the wrongs he did. This attribute of his is driven by his high pursuit for power which makes him defraud people easily for his benefit.

8. The blame can never be his

This guy is not brave enough to take the responsibility, so he pushes it. He will never own up to his wrong even if you catch him red-handed. There will always be a person to blame; sadly, that person may end up being you.

9. He has zero passion for people

Apologies are not so familiar with a sociopath and if you hear him apologize, know that he is not entirely truthful and that he wants to get something from you. He does not care if anyone is hurt, so he has no business having a rethink before or after defrauding a person. If you have him as a husband, then he will not care about your emotions in any way.

When he is narcissist

1. He is a celeb in his world

In the mind of a narcissist, he is a celebrity; because that is the only personality, he can imagine being comfortable. You will easily find him trying to deceive someone about this fact, and since he pictures himself as a celeb, there is no way he can live less. He will push and scramble for power and fame to prove that he truly exists.

Also, he can swear to his hurt that he is better and more unique than every other person. This man believes he is the best, and if he is a musician; he will tell you none other can play like he does. You will need special grace to handle a man like that.

2. He is entitled

It is either you give this brother of ours an individual treatment, or you are rude. He is entitled, and in his chicken mind, he deserves to be treated even better than the president (that is exaggerated). He feels he is better than the rest so he should not be treated like every other person. If this guy is your husband, he may want you to worship him in every aspect.

3. The attention must be his alone

You're staying in the relationship is determined by the amount of notice you give to this uncle. If you fail to feed him with it, he will kick you out and look for someone who can. This man will always need to be praised by friends and family, compliments, love and admiration is still the jacket they put on.

4. He has no time to be empathetic

He may never notice you are in pain because he does not have the time. He is so busy trying to get all the love and attention from you that he forgets to remember that you are bleeding. He does not also understand why people feel pity for others because he has never felt that way before.

5. He exaggerates

This man will tell you that the whole workplace stood in awe of him when he walked in due to his beautiful suit when in earnest; it was only one person that complimented his dressing. A narcissist will describe an ordinary life like an extraordinary one which he is always a superhuman.

When he is both

Having a person with any of these personality disorders can be challenging to handle; now, imagine if he is both. A narcissist sociopath is a person with the extremes of the two personalities, living with them can be very difficult and negatively criticizing them can trigger aggressive results. So when you have a narcissist sociopath, you need to be careful.

The following signs will tell you if your husband is suffering from the two personality disorders:

a) He will compliment you even when he does not mean it
b) He can insult others to make you feel better
c) They can get into everyone's circle because he knows how to adapt their behaviors
d) Conversations with him are boring as it will be all about him
e) He is super fabulous in bed; he has to prove to you that he is the best
f) Their charitable lifestyle only when it makes him look good in the eyes of people
g) He gets depressed from a little sadness, and he can stay in this state for some weeks

h) His relationships never ended well
i) They have no issues moving from one relationship to another

CHAPTER 3: Making a Decision

When we encounter difficulties in a relationship, the first thing that comes to our mind is to withdraw from it. This is because the mind feels that when it is absent from the cause of the pain, the pain will go. Sadly; this is not always true. The pain of heartbreak is usually challenging to cope.

Being married to a narcissist sociopath is not the worst thing on earth. Men like him have positive sides that can make marriage fun. So, before thinking of running away, consider the need to stay.

So, it is time to make a decision. This decision will depend on the effect of your husband's difficulty on you. If your husband cheats or abuses you (physically), leaving will be the right choice. Aside from this, staying with him will be better.

Reasons you should stay with your difficult husband

1. **It will soon get better**

Hard times come, but they do not last forever. It is okay to feel like quitting the relationship, but this may not always be the right option. Marriage is no child's play, and you just can't throw everything in the trash because of this. This hardness will not last forever. Soon, your husband will realize he was wrong and will change for the better; after all, the only permanent thing in life is change.

Though they may be no guarantee that a narcissist sociopath will get better, there is hope that he will someday let down his guard and allow you to influence his life till the marriage turns out sweet. When a man loves a woman, he will do everything to make her happy. Your narcissist sociopath husband can be that man, and you can be that woman.

No matter the difficulty you are experiencing now, have faith that better times will come, and when it does, you will look back at this time and be happy you stayed.

2. Love is a commitment

Leaving maybe the easy option now, but that does not mean it is the best. You may be frustrated with your husband, and you feel you want to end things. Think again, is that what you want deep down?

Your relationship is a long term one which has cost you so much time, energy and resources, so ending it should not be a rushed decision. It is always advisable to put in a little more effort and sew if the condition will not improve. Give yourself the time and give your husband the benefit of the doubt. Imagine if you pack your bags and leave now only to realize out there that you didn't honestly want to go. You will cause significant damage, maybe an irreparable one to your marriage.

So, instead of heading out the door in haste, take some more time and work things out with your husband. You never can tell, things may turn out better than you expected.

3. The longer you love, the more depth you have

Though calling it a quit seems easy and better now, hanging on and making it work together will give you more depth in love. You and your spouse will discover that you both love each other far better than you did before. Struggles bring more meaning to enjoy and overcoming the struggles makes the bond stronger.

I know it is tough to believe this now, but there is a great hope for your marriage. That so dark a cloud has a beautiful silver lining. I'm sure there are dragons you and your husband slain in your relationship. Slaying that means you can kill this, and slaying this means there will never be a dragon you and your spouse will never be able to slay together. It is too early and too late to give up.

4. You won't find fulfilment from someone new

it may be challenging to meet someone out there who will feel like your real soul mate, especially if you have spent some reasonable amount of time with your present partner. There are many things you two have learnt about each other right to make the relationship as secure as it is now. Starting again with another may not be that easy.

Do not think I'm flattering you to stay with your current partner; I am not; I'm only telling you the truth. Getting a new person will only bring you short term happiness. Many times, our problems are the mirrors that reflect our true selves and if you contributed in any way to the issue at hand, know that you will experience same if not worse with the new person. The sad thing will be that there will be no history like you had with your current partner to help you to hang on. This may keep you moving from one man to another, seeking for the fulfilment that only existed with your current partner.

If you are married to a narcissist sociopath, you may argue this point. But come to think of it, can you confidently say your husband has not improved on some aspect of his personality disorder? I believe he has because there is some level of influence that love has on a person. Do not rush for the new wine; the old one can still taste better. It just needs a little sweetening.

5. Love is a choice

Love is a commitment and marriage is a promise to be committed till death do you part. Love is a decision, and this decision does not only end on the first day, you have to make the decision every morning as you wake. Forget about the fairytale idea that you just fall in love and automatically stay fallen in it forever; no love is automatic. Love needs work, and as a married person, your work will not be hard; it will only be a decision to love your partner as long as you are awake.

The only quality reason to stay with your partner is because you love him. That is the only reason you will need to stay with any other person you can ever meet outside. Your husband may be a narcissist sociopath; you never can tell the one you will meet outside. We are different, and because of this, there will always be something to fight about. The love and the fight is what make a sweet relationship. There is an excellent chance of long-term joy if you choose to hang on.

CHAPTER 4: Surviving A Problematic Marriage

Choosing to stay in a good idea because in reality; most marriages go through really challenging and trying times. Overcoming these challenges is what transforms to being as fortunate as they are now. If your marriage is rocky right now, do not be in haste to live, you never know how good it can turn with a little effort.

Before we begin, I will want to believe that you and your husband loved each other at a point in your marriage. If you indeed did, then love can revive. However, if you had an arranged marriage or one based on a contract, you may have to consider the possibility of love seriously. You should do this before embarking on this journey.

Now we are on the same page; I guess we are good to go. Before we commence our fight for your marriage, I'll love you to know that you can only fight a good argument for your difficult marriage when you understand why your husband is difficult. This does not mean that every bad behavior must have a perfect explanation, it means that there if you get to see things from your husband's viewpoint, items can be better.

We already know that a narcissist sociopath is born to be difficult so we will not go into the causes for his difficulty. His personality causes his problem, and there is little or nothing you can do about it as a wife.

So now why are some husbands with great personalities difficult?

Why your supposedly wonderful husband may be difficult

There are many reasons men become difficult; some may be purely innocent, while others may be from cockiness or lack of proper home training. While considering the reasons our husbands may be difficult, we should get to understand that our husbands may be just as worried as we are about this issue. What I mean is that your husband Y not have an idea why you say he is difficult and so cannot place why you keep bringing up the same topic every time.

When his ambiguous attitude is your fault

Before putting all the blame on your darling husband for being difficult, know that you caused it We ladies have a way of pushing men away with our behaviors, not because you ate wrong but because his macho mind thinks you should not be the one telling him what to do. Now let's are how we push our husbands to become the men they are to be:

- **You are too concerned**

When you were both unmarried, you were independent, and your husband had the freedom to do what he pleased. No one loves to be controlled or excessively accountable. In the early years of marriage, a man may find it difficult to tell you everything or ask for your opinion before making any decisions. You can't say he does not love you; he does, he just needs time to adjust to the married life.

Being too concerned about where he is or where he went to may push him away and cause him to be defensive in the marriage. It is dangerous to force your husband to this level. You may be innocent in your concern; it may be out of love, but your husband may not see it that way. Being too concerned may choke your husband; do not think it is a show of appreciation.

Get back to the independent life and go on minding your business. When you two meet at the end of the day, you two can talk about your day. If you ask him for anything and he feels too uncomfortable to answer, leave him. He may not be in the mood to talk much.

- **You place your family or the children first**

Men are jealous; they are even jealous of their children. When a man perceives that you value your family or the children more than him, he'll start acting up. Some subtle men may try to distract you from the children or may even do things to get our attention. Sadly, we may not notice their effort. If this happens in your home, it may lead your husband into feeling like you have lost the love you have for him (poor him!). A man that feels unloved can be rebellious and difficult.

This cause of difficulty is not a difficult one to handle. All you need do is to give him more attention. Before this, ensure you do something romantic (like giving him a back scrub or giving him a special treat when the children are not around) and apologize for losing your focus on him. Remind him that you love and value him and all his efforts.

Men are boys on the inside; it's not that hard to get to their soft spot. Understand your husband that is your first role as a wife and keep his heart with you. When his heart is in yours, and you consciously include him in the jokes, he will feel wanted.

- **You two barely agree**

Continuous disagreements sap the joy out of marriage. If you and your spouse find it hard to decide over many issues, he may lose his love for you.

Marriage is the union that combines people of different views and values with different upbringing together. You and your husband have different minds and opinions about various subjects, and your marriage may never grow till you two learn to compromise.

Compromise is not entirely letting go of your values; it is finding a midpoint between your costs and that of your husband. Get your husband to understand this fact, and if he does not, I recommend you talk to a counsellor.

- **You do not trust his judgments**

Lack of trust in any part can make marriage difficult. If you do this, then your husband considers you as tricky as you find him. He may not be perfect, but there is no harm in trusting him.

He may be cocky and unwilling to listen to you (even when he knows you are right); that is men for you. So once in a while, allow him to dance his way, and when he cries back to you (which we know he will), you welcome him with a pat on the back (not a nag).

- **You said it more than once**

You know what he calls a nag? Telling him not to forget his ulcer drugs so that his intestines don't get chewed up because you are 101% sure that he will forget it. It's hard to stop, especially when you know that your fear will come true. But what can you do? Say it once, after that; it is a nag.

If you get as hooked up as I am where my family is concerned, I'll advise you to get a little less concerned. Do not remind him about your son's sports day at school; you can say it once if you didn't say it in the last two days. When his son refuses to give him that warm hug when he is back from work, he will understand that your reminders are essential.

At the end, you will have a man whose ears are yours; your health will be in good shape (since the nutrients you take are nourishing your body instead of replacing the lost energy from nagging)

When his ambiguous attitude is his fault:

- **You are all he has**

It is funny how men tend to protect the only precious thing they have. When a man loves you to a fault, he will want to protect you by all means. This may cause him to be controlling and demanding.

If this case sounds like yours, then do not complain by facing him off. He believes he is doing what he is for your good and facing him off will make him feel you are unappreciative or you do not love him. When he feels this way, he will pull back.

Instead of comforting him, gently talk to him about the way his controlling behavior makes you feel. You know you own his heart, so a sweet talk that sinks his soul will make him have a rethink.

- **He is busy**

If your husband always forgets to tell you things, it could be because he is knowledgeable and always busy. Funny; right? Yes, intelligent men are always trying to figure out a lot of things, and so they tend to forget the things that matter the most.

In a case like this, there is nothing much you can do. Just look at his praiseworthy side (the intelligence or hard work) and learn to appreciate it.

A busy and successful man needs a supportive woman who will understand his position and fill in the gap for him. Though you may not understand his reasons for some actions, trust him and wait till the time is right; I'm sure he will tell them to you.

If you are supportive, his love for you will escalate, and he will find you irresistible.

- **He feels entitled**

This is bad, and it is terrible to have an entitled husband. He may be challenging to please, and this can be so disheartening for you as his wife. The most typical classes of men that do this are the mama's boys; they will expect you to be nothing less than their mothers. Sad!

Oh, dear! I earnestly pray that you marry a man who loves you for being you and not trying to convert you into mothering him and his children at the same time.

So how do you know your husband is entitled? It is simple; he whines about everything and tries to get them his way. He is never satisfied with what you offer and will always have preferences for something else.

For this kind of man, you may never do enough so instead of killing yourself to make him see that you are right, withdraw. Do your best and leave the rest.

When he can't get them, and when he sees you do not care whether he is happy or not, he will start chasing you again. Here, you will have the opportunity to correct things to the way you want. Isn't that sweet?

- **He has some unprocessed issues**

There are times when your husband will not tell you all of his challenges. That time maybe every time. He will always try to figure some things by himself to prevent you from being bothered.

We have to learn to spot this time and give him the space he desires. Continually asking him what the problem is may cause him to be irritated, he may even shout at you or push you away.

Know when to speak. Let him deal with his issues the way he seems fit, and if he needs your help, he'll ask. Take the time to make yourself happy.

CHAPTER 5: Making It Work With Your Difficult Spouse

According to newton's law of inertia, a body will continue in its continuous state of rest or constant speed in a straight line motion until a force is applied on it. This means that your marriage will continue in that path of difficulty until you decide to push for a change. so sitting down with folded hands and tears in your eyes won't get you the husband of your dreams; doing these will:

Get the right mindset for a successful marriage

The right mindset for marriage is what will keep you even when you are married to a narcissist sociopath. This is because you know what marriage is and have made up your mind to live happily in marriage whether or not it is the kind you needed.

The following will help you develop the right mindset that makes marriage works.

1. **Understand that love is commitment**

This is where you will draw your strength. Love is war and to stay in your marriage, you have to fight. The only thing is that you will fight for the union and not fighting it. This is a part most people do not understand. Daily, we fight our marriages with the evil thoughts and bad words. This is very common when the marriage is going through a rough time.

Right now, about 50% of marriages in America will end in divorce; this is pathetic for the marriage ministry. And if 30% of couples getting involved were to understand that love is a commitment and that they have to fight to stay married, then the rate of expected divorce will reduce by 30 %.

Every marriage has passed through its fire; the only difference is what fueled their fire. If you have the rare opportunity of having happily married parents, please ask them how they got to the place they are. They will tell you that there were times their marriage was so tricky till they felt like giving up. This is the most significant confirmation we need. If they could make it; you too can. And even if they could not; your case will be different.

2. **Know that as long as you live, 'life' will always happen**

John Lennon said, "life is what happens when you are busy making other plans", and this is so true. Life happens to everybody. We get fired when we are having plans on how to get better at the job; the car breaks down when we are getting late for the trip, and marriage to becomes complicated when we are preparing a bed of roses. It happens; life happens.

So what do we do when life hits our marriages hard? Join the 50% of Americans who are breaking off their marriages in court? No way! We fight and one of the ways to fight well is to have this mindset that life happens. Now, what is life?

Life is the margin that differentiates the living from the dead. It is a force, and its characteristics are growth, metabolism, reproduction, constant adaptation through internal change and even the ability to react.

So there are times your marriage wants to grow, and we both know that most period of growth are not always funny. Ever experience the pain of a growing wisdom tooth? Oh, dear! If you have, you will develop some patience while your marriage goes through the normal process of growth.

During this period of growth, all you need do is to be prayerful (if you believe in prayers) and be the best you can. Love your spouse unconditionally if you can (because that does not sound achievable, but what's the harm if you try?); refuse to fight, and carefully learn to do the steps coming after this.

3. **Change your perception about the marriage**

Life ends where challenges end, and as long as your marriage is still living, problems will always come. The difference between a union that will stand the test of time and the one that will end in court just like the other 50% is how the individuals involved view challenges.

Here is the bitter truth; you may never be able to get your spouse to stop being difficult entirely; you may never even be able to get him to give up on that problematic character. However, you can shield yourself and your marriage from the effect of his difficult actions.

I know our husbands' actions can hurt us, but after carefully studying the word "hurt", I got to realize that we get hurt because we allow ourselves.

4. **Believe you have the key**

We are the women, and we have the key to either build or destroy our marriages. Marriages don't die except the owner allows it. To your husband, he thinks he is a good man and playing his role to keep the home (do not argue, even if it's not right, let's assume it is), so it is solely dependent on you to build the marriage.

Here is what I mean. If your husband believes he is doing the right thing and you indeed do the right thing on your path, what do you think will happen? Peace will reign. Being provoked to anger whenever your husband makes a terrible decision without even thinking it would have been a good thing to have consulted, you will not bring peace. It will only take away your peace.

So, know that the key to a happy marriage is right in your hands. You decide what you do with it. Also, do not forget that the key to a terrible marriage and divorce is also in your hands. I hope you throw that key far away so that you will never lay your hands on it. A bad marriage is not a thing to wish anyone.

Make him the man

A man can be anything for the woman he loves. So how can you be sure he still loves you?

Years may have passed, but your man's love can even make him do the things he did for you when you were dating. So, let's help you revive that love you have missed for a long time.

1. Pick up your glow

It is a common thing to see women lose their glow after some years in marriage. This should not be so, but despite how we try, our beauty can still go down when we no longer get the joy we deserve from our marriages. This may be you, but if it is not; then I am honestly glad for you.

Get back to your makeup box, throw out the expired ones (because some of them may have been there since you were single) and teach yourself how to look good again. Always try to be the first representation of yourself. Look good; let your husband be drawn back to that stunning beauty again. You need his attention to get this thing straightened out.

Your husband will be reminded of the girl he fell for when you first met, and his heart will be tender. With a tender heart, you can present your case and expect a good turn around.

2. Submit to him

I don't know what the word submission means to you, but I know that the only thing in this life that has two heads is what we call "a monster". So, if you want your home to become monstrous, become the second head.

Look! I know that was direct and somewhat rude because of the world we live in now. Many women are going the feminist way and trying to be equal to the man. That will not be so helpful here. It is okay to seek to be treated with respect but trying to be a man (play his role or teach him what to do) when there is a man at home will bring you only one thing; war!

Men feel at ease when they believe that they have the loyalty and respect of their wives; even narcissist sociopaths do. This confidence allows them to let down their guard and be open to suggestions. Without this, a man will try to prove his authority by enacting rules without having a second thought since he wants his wife to know that he is the man. You know what, he will prove that to you, and you will feel the pains.

So instead of allowing your man to prove his authority and inflict pains on you, why not just let him be the man, lose his guard and lay all his strength on your laps? There is strength in being weak, and there is a weakness in strength. Do not let the false power of the world's standard (that is sending 50% of couples their separate ways) affect yours.

CHAPTER 6: Making Marriage With A Narcissist Sociopath Work

There is a powerful way to break the wings of your sociopath husband. This is usually the most comfortable way out. People seem to change as they age but doing the right thing may get him to have a rethink about his actions sooner than later.

Retaining your joy

1. **Examine how you feel and write them down**

A narcissist sociopath will do everything in his power to make you feel less. He will still complain you burnt the pancakes even when they are perfectly fine. When actions like this continue, it can make you feel awkward.

The way to draw strength is to examine how his actions make you feel and name it. For instance, when he complains about the burnt pancakes, he trying to make you feel bad for something you never did. In that case, you can say that he is trying to make you feel guilty. When you name the feeling, you will be able to learn how you can get over it.

2. Find the triggers

The triggers are the things he says or does that makes you feel the way you do. You can keep yourself from falling into his trap when you learn and retain the triggers at your fingertips. That way, you will always be hopeful of his actions. Find the triggers and develop your immunity against his effects and refuse to be taken by surprise.

3. Refuse to feel guilty

Refuse to "buy into that". Your husband only succeeds at making you feel guilty when he gets you to buy into the guilt. But if you consciously or subconsciously refuse to buy into the guilt, he will fail in this mission. Even if you burnt the pancakes, refuse to feel guilty. Accidents happen, and people mistakenly burn dinners; that does not mean they are bad people. You are not a bad person so refuse to feel like you are. The person to feel guilty is your husband because he threw his temper at you for just a little mistake (which you may or may not have made).

The decision is yours. You can choose to feel the way your husband wants you to, or you can take charge of your emotions. It is possible to stay guilt-free even when everything around you is trying to make you feel that way.

4. Define the situation

The best way to stay guilt-free when married to a narcissist sociopath is to define the situation. Take your mind back to what truly happened and see if you were indeed at fault. Remember when you way making the pancakes; did they look burnt to you? You know you made it to specially suit his taste and the fact that he refused to appreciate it does not mean you did not play your role.

CHAPTER 7: Can Marriage To A Narcissist Sociopath Husband Ever Get Better? - How To Make It Work

Of course! A marriage can get better even when you are married to the devil. Love changes people, and a narcissist sociopath can be one of the. However, before marriage with this kind of man gets better, some tough work must be done.

A sociopath has his weaknesses, and these weaknesses and anyone who can harness these weaknesses can ultimately win him over. Here is how you can fix the perfect one:

a) Do not criticize him

You will only worsen things with a narcissist sociopath when you criticize him. Do not forget, he is accurate and will not smile at anyone that tries to prove him otherwise. Criticizing him is like fighting against him; you will never win. Instead, you will get a very terrible reaction from him. The key to dealing with a sociopath is carefulness with every statement you make.

b) Use his ego for your good

He has the pride and since you cannot fight it, feed it. He believes he is the best, so make him feel he is and get yourself some peace. Since his hands can be too tight to release resources, you can praise him till his hands gradually get open.

c) Validate him

The primary reason a narcissist sociopath acts the way he does is to prove his importance in a place. Now, if you praise him and reassure him of his significance as the head of the family, he will not need to go the extra mile to prove himself. So when next you want to talk to your narcissist sociopath husband and get his full attention and empathy, start with phrases like "I don't know what we would have done in this home without you…" or "you are the best thing that has happened to us that is why…" etc.

d) Start with an apology

Since his actions are always bent on getting you to feel bad and apologize, relieve him of the stress by apologizing before starting the conversation. This will make him find it needless to push you to the corner since he has already gotten the needed apology.

CHAPTER 8: Guide To Being The Submissive Wife

To win your husband, you do not have to fake the submission. Be submissive for real else, you will be tired of wearing a mask, and your true self will show. If you have some challenges with understanding what the proper submission is, then follow our guide to being the submissive wife below.

a) **Improve in the areas you are not so good at**

If your husband were to have an opportunity to say the things you do that makes him feel uncomfortable, you would be surprised. Remember, some men take up being difficult as a reactive measure to the things you do to hurt their pride. If this is the reason they are challenging, then they will be softened when they see a genuine change.

Ask your husband the parts he does not feel so comfortable about in you; tell him you think wrong about demeaning him with your character, and so you want to change. Allow him enough time to think and give you a reply. When he does, try to get better. By so doing, he will be encouraged to drop some of the things you complain.

However, if your husband is a narcissist sociopath, he may never stop being the person he is. So in that case, improve yourself but not for him. You have your life to live, and the actions of a man cannot hinder your joy.

b) Keep your mouth shut so that a blaming word does not slip out

We ladies have always used our mouths to destroy our homes. It is so sad how the little tongue can break down to nothing what we used decades to build. When dealing with a difficult husband, keeping your mouth closed is always the first line of action. This does not mean you should not talk about the behavior or anything; it means you should not say a word when either of you is angry.

Talking when any of you is angry will not bring a solution. It will only bring a fight and engaging in that fight is a sign that you are weak. Yeah! Am I touching your button? Now, real strength is displayed by keeping quiet when every part of you wants to scream. Also, fighting with your husband will make him feel disrespected. When you make a man feels this way, get ready to see his worst side.

As a married couple, there is always a good time to talk. For most people, that time is the night, and for the remaining few, they know when it is suitable. You must have been able to identify the best time to talk to your husband. If you didn't; then find a time when he is less busy, happy and with a full stomach to talk.

c) Be gracious

Being gracious has to do with having a quiet and gentle spirit. To be silent does not mean losing your stands or being mute. It does not mean being easily pushed and tossed. It means being confident in yourself without having to prove yourself to anyone. Now, this is the definition of class. So when I say be gracious, I mean **BE CLASSY!**

With class, no man, not even the one you submit to can override you. To be classy means you are quiet but articulate and persuasive when presenting your reasons. She does not have to scream and shout to be heard; she is heard even without saying a word! You feel that? That can be you.

You can achieve this by being at peace with yourself. Get something (aside from your husband) that makes your life meaningful. Do something new; do something that makes you happy. Those things will help you let go of the anger your husband's attitude was to have on you.

d) Choose your battle

Fighting every battle will wear you out. There may be many things that make your husband difficult, but you do not have to tackle all of them. Pick what is most pressing and handle. Let the others go till you are ready to face them. You can address his refusal to provide when you are sure he didn't lose his job a week ago.

When you have a difficult husband, you will find everything he does to be offensive. Keeping up with all his misdeeds will only turn you into a nag. Nagging will not get you the marriage you want. It will only drive your husband out of the home. Do not think that will bring you peace. No dear, it won't. It will bring you a home without a head and your children, no father to call their own.

Instead of spending all your energy fighting a man who doesn't see anything wrong with what he is doing, channel it to doing the things you love. Do them will the same fierce energy; you will be surprise at the result you will get and the joy it will bring.

e) Keep your cool and do the right thing

We are often tempted to do the wrong thing because our husbands just don't want to do it right. Remember, you are a different person. The fact that he makes life difficult for you does not mean you have to feed him with the food he has prepared. No, if he is so hungry for it, he will feed himself.

He is the difficult one, not you; so stay good for yourself and your kids. Even if you wanted to pay him back with his coin, how will that benefit you? It will give you a moment of happiness but after that, what next? I know it may be challenging to overcome the temptation, especially when he keeps doing it every time. So when he misbehaves again, remember this:

- Your anger will hurt you and your children more
- You will be dancing according to his tune by repaying him evil for evil. You are better than that; never do the things below your standards.

- Anger will hurt your liver, so keeping the hurt in remembrance to plan a payback will only deteriorate your health.
- Your husband knows what will get you pissed. So, when you refuse to fight back, he will have nothing to be defensive about when you ignore his misdeeds. With that, he will feel stupid and surrender.

Conclusion

You must be familiar with the phrase "marriage is not a bed of roses". It may be true that marriage is not a bed of roses, but we can always rip out the thorns and make our marriage a bed of beautiful flowers (since it cannot be roses); and in cases where we cannot, we find a way to get around with the thorns.

Marriages can be successful if one partner chooses to fight for it. You are here because you want to fight for your marriage and your choice is not a mistake.

It does not matter the kind of man you got married to; you will find joy in the marriage. This is because your happiness will not be dependent on your husband or the situations surrounding your marriage; your joy is in you, and nothing can take that away from you.

Printed in Great Britain
by Amazon